leave the light on when you go

star hands

leave the light on, when you go

DEDICATION

To my younger self, you still have so much waiting for you.

Authors note: all poems in this book are works of fiction, none of these works are meant to encourage any type of behavior and are purely meant for education, awareness, comfort, and perspective.

star hands

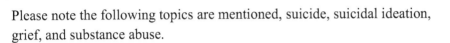

Please note the following topics are mentioned, suicide, suicidal ideation, grief, and substance abuse.

please reach out if you are struggling, some resources are below, so do not hesitate to reach out, to loved ones, a stranger on a crisis line, or further sort of mental health professional.

let your loved ones know you love them, check up on them, and remind them there is help. it is better to have an awkward conversation, leading to getting help than to lose someone.

remember that there is always someone willing to help you, you do not have to be alone.

988 — United States suicide hotline (English and Spanish)

1 (833) 456 4566 — Canada's suicide hotline

0800 689 5652 —- UK's suicide hotline

131114 —- Australia's suicide hotline

CONTENTS

watching the sun on the beach disappear into the water

a list of everything I want

I want to never come back to my hometown after I leave it. I want to die in it.
I want to be ten. I want to be eleven, six, seven and eight. I want freedom.
I want to wear shorts in the summertime and not consider the scars.
I want water balloon fights, and
I want to give out Halloween candy to the neighborhood kids.
I want to never speak to my mother again,
and I want to hold her hand in her final moments.
I want to be her daughter, I want to be her son,
I want to be something she is proud to call her own.
I want her to never find out where I have moved to,
and I want a multi-generational house.
I want to forget my mother, and I'm scared
there will come a day she won't remember me anymore.

I want children. I want to live alone.
I want to be a father; I want to be a mother.
I want to brush my daughter's hair gentler than mine,
and I want her to wear the same onesies my mom kept.
I want her to have my mother's last name
and her mother's first name as her middle name.
I want her to never feel like she's on her own beneath my roof.
I want her to look out into the night,
and be reminded no matter how far she is, I am only a call away.
I want to have home videos my son can look back on.
I want him to know he is my sun.
I want to watch him build his life, and I want him to know
I am proud of him every single day.
I want to carry my child on my shoulders and
I want to point to the constellations, naming them all right,
I want to tell them there is one unnamed, and it is theirs to call their own.

I want to marry some guy I met in high school who has a boring last name,
like Smith or Johnson, or some girl whose heart is far more open than my
own I met in college, in some kind of movie way, the way that makes others
believe love still exists.

I want a girl who loves me like she doesn't know gentle hands still have nails.
I want her to remind me I am alive.
I want her to love me so harshly and beautifully. I have no choice but to
become religious, I want her to give me faith I am afraid of.
I want her to love me like a dog,
so, I can know why I didn't leave when it was me.

star hands

I want a boy who loves me quietly, who is shy when he asks to kiss me.
I want a husband; I want a wife. I want a girlfriend; I want a boyfriend.
I want to be the love of someone's life.
I want to be somebody's someone.
I want it to be you.

I want to move in with my friends and I want to never live a day alone again.
I want a tiny sunlit house, only one of everything
because it's just me and a dog.
I want a busy schedule, and I want to go out
on a wednesday afternoon to the store, or movies.
I want to be a writer, full-time. I want to be good enough to have burnout.
I want someone to look back at my work, fifty, eighty,
a hundred and ten years from now, and think,
"we would've been good friends if I knew you then."
I want to be on the other side of the "you saved my life,"
comments, and messages.

I want to understand myself, not for reconstruction but for pure interest.
I want to know myself, so I can know if I am good enough,
if the praise is only surface level.

I want to be surface level, I want to be mediocre,
so, I have an excuse to give up.
I want to go to an art college; I want to be able to pay for it in cash.
I want money. I want to be a teacher, high school, or college professor.
I want to like loud environments.
I want to be an extrovert; I want to like who I am when I am not alone.
I want to have a voice that feels like my art,
I want a voice that could carry the weight of my heart.
I want a body that I can look at and not wonder
if everyone I have ever loved had only felt pity for me.
I want to be my biggest enemy.
I want to get to myself first, so, when other people do
at least I already accepted that.

I want to not be queer; I want to not be me; I want to be me.
I want to be a man; I want to be a woman or something in between—
I can't easily explain in a casual conversation.
I want to be a drag queen, and I want my grandmother
to call me her grandson.

I want to transition in the country I was raised in,
I want my real name next to my poetry.

I want my friends and I to grow old in the bodies
we have reclaimed as our own.
I want a world where a life like mine,
which may have been only a phase for others is even possible to consider.
I want to read poetry about transitioning as a person of color,
I want to look up to someone who looks like me.
I want to meet people from every walk of life who are like me.
I want to have a life I want to live.
I want a world I am not horrified to wake up in.
when people speak about my life after I am gone.
I want them to not hesitate to say I was queer.
I don't want them to set it aside, and brush it over, it is not entirely who I am,
but it is a fundamental part of my life that I can't separate myself from.
I want the ability to control choices made about my body.
I want snow days, and I want a world to wake up in.
I want to see the modern world to be modern,
I want to see change from what we have said to have learned from.
I want a future to look towards, and I want a family
and the dream I was raised on, that they said they swore for us
when we learned the words to the promise in pre-school.

I want to be who my mother had fought for me to be able to be.
I want to be a teenage girl and someone's beautiful baby boy.
I want to rip out my hair and I want curls.
I want to be normal; I want to not wake up one day
and randomly want to die all over again.
I want my months of progress to not feel meaningless
every time I get bad again.
I want to kill myself and I want to be a success story
that tells of all the ugly the beauty conceals.
I want to get bad again. I want to get better, so I can write every day again.
I want to drown myself, and I want to be able to float
without giving in to the urge to look down.

I want to know what's wrong with me, and I want to still be interesting.
I want to die at twenty. I want to see the twenty-second century.

I want to live in some place I've never been.
I want get a medical, law, or engineering degree,
something that matters for the time being.
I want to be an astronaut, astrophysicist, and tarot card reader.

I want to be a musician—it's a better chance of a job in the arts
because it's what I promised myself I'd do with my life.

4

star hands

I want my fortune read, I want to believe in god, I want heaven to exist.
I want to be a doctor, I want to save lives, and truly know
I have changed someone's life.

I want to never leave my house again.
I want to see the world and find something to miss when I die.
I want to delete all my socials and start all over. personal and creative.
I want to be famous, selfishly, I want people to see my name in lights,
I want to know that I matter, beyond a tiny pool of names I have memorized.
I want my words quoted and my verses in anthologies,
I want to be remembered.
I want my face to be recognizable, I want to be analyzed, I want to never die.
I want someone to not know me personally
but feel as if I am a friend, someone who understands.

I want the people who know me personally,
to never catch me in a state of vulnerability.

I want a quiet death, in my sleep.
I want to think that the sunset that occurred after was probably not as good
as the ones I've seen, and what a shame it is I couldn't photograph it,
I want to think someone missed it for me.
I want to remember to look both ways when I cross the street.
I want to learn everything again,
and I want to know if it all works out in the end.
I want to know what I can't, and I want to lose what I don't have.
I want to start over, and I want to know the end.

leave the light on, when you go

you are Neil

you are five years old, going through the car wash for the first time.
the bright colors make you think of what your first teenage party will be like,
what song will they play?
will it ever compare to the feeling of listening to your parent's radio
as they sing along on a trip to the store?

you are seven years old, with lemonade dripping from your lips,
the cold rushes into your stomach and the sun beams gently onto your body.
you believe that god is real, or at least you don't care if he isn't.
you have not yet been to a funeral, so you still believe that
death is a faraway time, like the year you graduate, like Friday,
your birthday, winter when it's summer.
but right now, today is none of those days.
today is not like any other day, because it will last forever.
for now, time doesn't matter; infinity is the highest number you can count to.
you are a child, and when the day falls into the night,
your father will carry you to bed, and your mother will be there
when you wake in the morning.

you are ten years old, you have been to a funeral now,
and instead of feeling sad thinking about how long you have left
with the people you love, you begin to say, "I love you" twice
before leaving the house, hug your friends more often before they go,
and try to compliment people when you used to be scared to talk to strangers.

you are fourteen, and you know what being trans is.
you didn't get to have the boyhood that the other boys had,
but that's about finding yourself, and I can assure you,
you have plenty of time.
you still have a long way to go.
you know who you are—nobody can take that from you.
people can deny your existence,
but they'll never be able to kill the star in your heart.
when you think about the feeling of the sun on your chest
and the beach breeze, you swear, heaven exists on the tip of your tongue.

all the years you spent rotting away in your bedroom
wondering what was wrong with you have become a little easier
to understand as you look back on them now.
someday you will make a home out of the body you were given,
and you will be proud, even despite what they may do or say.
you have to live for yourself because nobody else goes when you do.

star hands

you are fifteen, with another boy in your arms.
his heartbeat feels as gentle as the petals of a flower, and you feel free
like a child running through sprinklers. the moment feels infinite.
you do not want morning to come, because the sound of his voice is far
sweeter than any lullaby the birds can offer,
but don't worry, he'll still be there tomorrow.
sometimes time slows enough, you begin to think it never began
until it slips through your hand.

so, hold on to this moment, as you drift off into sleep;
you'll never be this you again, he will never be this version of himself again.
however, the love you feel will last your whole life,
all the love that came from you— all the love given to you—is yours to keep.
this is your life, the only one you will ever have.
there is still time to love, discover yourself,
and be who you are afraid to be,
but there is not forever.

leave the light on, when you go

beautiful boy

my legs lay on the bed, I'm looking ahead at my desk.
I say, "I feel like I think better when I lay like this."
you laugh and get into the same position next to me,
but instead of looking forward, your eyes stay fixated on me.

"I wish we weren't so young. then I could have a life with you," I say.
you stay quiet but give me a soft smile.

"we could have a garden full of roses, all colors, but red especially." I pause.
"and, a cat, actually no, two, or three, and a dog, not like a big one,
but a small one or medium, maybe."

my eyes stay fixated ahead, you listen intently,
seeing the fantasy play out like a movie.

"and we could have a sunlit kitchen, and I could make you breakfast in bed,
and wash your hair when you're tired and we could write together, make art,
you could find scary movies for us to watch if you promise to not let me sleep
alone."

you see the kitchen and see us standing in front of the coffee maker
some far years from now, but the fantasy is too faint to tell if it's soon to be
memories or merely a dream, barely out of reach.

I ask you, as my hand brushes against yours with a milk carton in my hand,
"would you like sugar or milk?" and we laugh,
because I already know, I've known for years.
but I can never seem to figure out what to say
before the words come spilling out of my mouth.

around you, I'm someone else, I learn a part of myself I've long forgotten.
I don't know if I want to know it, but you already do.
I recognize it, within myself, we find familiarity in each other,
as if we had known each other our whole lives.

"we could get away from how complicated everything is now, I hope,
and we could have a place that doesn't know the anger we grew up with,
a quiet warm house, always with food, and always welcome."
I wait for a response this time.
"I'd like that," you finally say.

star hands

"get married for the benefits then go out to our favorite restaurant," I add.

"you better make a good proposal. don't think just because we're not in love
that you don't have to give me a fairytale," you say through a laugh.

"of course, I'd do anything for you," I stop for a second.
"I love you, you're my best friend."

you laugh, but you've only made out bits and pieces of what I have said.
the fantasy is still faintly playing out in your mind,
it plays on rewind that night.

for years it seems, you wish that you had done something different, said what
you really thought about the life we could build, how maybe even though
we're young we could figure out how to make it work,
like we always had before.

back then all we had was ourselves, we didn't know each other yet,
but we always hoped we'd meet someone like us,
someone who would understand.

I imagine what we could do as a team,
we'd never have to carry the weight alone again.
we could keep each other safe; we could be alright
if we weren't alone tonight, I'm sure, the future would find its way to us.

for years it seems you wonder
if you have now made a mistake, you can't take back.
you wonder if the familiarity you found in me is a warning sign,
you wonder if you are too much of your mother's child to fall,
too independent to depend on anyone else.
you wonder if your father's anger is a repulsion to love
if you'll grow into your brother's shoes.

when I drift off to sleep, I feel the gentle brush of fingertips against my
cheek. you sweetly speak to me, but I can barely make out the words.
as I stare at your lips, the whole world seems to grow quieter.
I swear I can feel my heart beat faster as the inches between us
change to centimeters, then only a few moments away, I close my eyes
and the feeling is nothing like I've ever known before.
still, I'm never unsure of it, but before I can open my eyes again,
the mourning doves have already started singing.

leave the light on, when you go

a cycle stuck on repeat

he sits at the bar, the same one his father used to go to when they still talked,
but he always said he'd never be anything like him.
when he nearly finishes his glass, he wonders about his father:
if he had thought about his wife and his kids when he reached the end,
or when he thought of them, did they make the drink taste stronger or weaker
did he down it faster or slower with them in mind?
he often wondered if he was to blame.
he had his younger brother, but he wasn't very good at making friends,
so, his best company has always been himself; the friends he did have made
him feel like he was staring at a mirror, with someone pointing out every
insecurity, some of which he didn't even know he had before, but now he has.
when he was sixteen, he had a girlfriend, they were on and off.
she only liked cigarettes, at first; she just hung around those people
because she liked the smell of smoke.
but one night, at a time when she thought the night was darker
than sunlight could outshine the next morning, she got one and lit it.
then one every so often, then one every other day,
and then a couple of times a day.
then she switched what she was using, a few times multiple different
substances, the next worse than the last.
he's not even sure of what she was doing the night it took her.

he found her; she was on his bathroom floor.
she was there because she said she wanted him to help her get sober.
he was almost positive she didn't have anything on her,
that when she came to his house, she was clean, but he wasn't sure enough.
he knew he couldn't help her on his own, so, the next morning
he was supposed to drive her to her mother's house.
she wanted to explain everything to her before anything,
in person, herself before she left.
his ex-girlfriend said her mother being told what her daughter had been
doing by someone else would break her heart, her mother would blame
herself and ask what she could have done, but at least this way her daughter
could explain that it wasn't her mother's fault
and comfort her before she had to leave.
he was the one who told her mother,
and the look on her face made him afraid to ever be a father.
the thought that his kids could be too scared of what he'd think of them
to get help, that he could lose them
and not have been able to do anything to save them.

after he's finished a few drinks,
he thinks now's the time to put his plan into action.
he refined every detail a couple of times over by now, it's almost memory.
he asks the bartender for a napkin,
and the businessman sitting next to him for a pen.
he wonders how many people he used to know will go to work tomorrow,
unaffected by his absence.
he scribbles down a number, and he walks out with the napkin in his pocket.
he calls a friend, and they drink a bit more at his house,
and when his friend is asleep, he goes into the kitchen.

the house is quiet, it never was like that when he was a kid,
but he swore he'd be the change.

CALL DURATION: 1:12

he stutters and his voice is shaky.
"Hello, is this Neil's mother?"

she is soft-spoken but any emotion is easily heard in her voice,
"Yes, who are you?"

"Alex, a friend of Neil's. I don't know if you remember me."

"Oh, Alex, I haven't heard from you in a while.
Is there a reason you're calling and on Neil's phone?
Are you two alright?"

"Hello?"

"Alex, has something happened?"

"I'm sorry, I can't do this. I'll have the hospital call you, I am sorry.
Catherine, he loved you. You were a great mom. It was nice knowing you all,
and Neil, knowing him—shit, they're here now, I'm sorry, it's my fault—"

CALL END

his friend sits on the curb outside as the police ask for more information.
his words are slurred, and his voice keeps breaking,
tears streaming down his face.
he hasn't cried like in years, and the last time he did, Neil was there.
he was there after Neil's girlfriend passed;
he watched him throw up in the bathroom at the funeral.

when he finally can speak, he says,
"the signs were there. I wish I saw them then."
he brushes away the tears still falling down his face one by one,
but he can't keep up.

"I wish he talked to me; I wish that I had brought it up with him."
"we used to be closer. maybe if we still were,
he would have reached out to me."

after the police leave, the hospital calls Neil's family.
the funeral comes and passes.

Alex walks alone downtown. he passes the bar; cigarette butts are littered
on the pavement in front of the door making him turn his head away.
he looks for his friend's face in every crowd, but he's never there.

none of them have his voice, not even his father.
Alex met him once or twice when they were kids.
he had a scruffy dark brown beard back then; now he's got a long one,
with a few gray hairs littered.

Neil said he'd never grow into his father but never acknowledged what he
went through as a kid because of his father, he made the same mistakes,
only in a different way, a sooner ending,
maybe if he wasn't so scared of what his mother would think of him
when her little boy began to follow his father's steps,
he would have reached out for help.

Neil's brother, Peter, graduates middle school today.
Alex came, in his place, but he feels guilty
looking around at all the supporting parents, grandparents, and siblings
when he's just a friend of someone who used to be a brother.

Peter's face lights up when he sees him and runs to hug him.

"I didn't think you'd want to come!"

"of course, I would. you've gotten so tall—soon you'll be taller than me."

Neil was taller than Alex.
He always poked fun at that fact since he was younger than Alex
by two years.

Peter looks just like Neil did when they first met.

only this time he hopes, he can save him.
Alex wasn't there when Neil needed him,
but he can be there if Peter does and if he is there,
maybe he can be the help Neil needed, maybe he can be the one to stop him
from ever getting close to where Neil had been.
if he stayed around maybe he could save him this time,
keep some part of his friend alive, he could see Peter get the life
Neil wanted to show him he could have once he got out of that house.

Peter sits there with his friend,
waiting for his name to be called and to get his hand shaken,
as the names go from A to Z, he remembers being told by somebody,
that not all his classmates would make it to high school graduation.
ever since he lost his brother, he's started holding onto time with his loved
ones like it's running, but he thinks he's realized no matter how much he
spends with someone there's a next time for it's never enough
for someone he can never say, *"see you later,"* to again.

by the end of the ceremony,
his classmates are restless and chatting with each other.
someone asks him what he wants to be when he grows up,
and he says a writer.
they ask him what he would write about, and he says, his brother
because he doesn't want anyone to feel as alone as he did.
if he could just save one life, and spare one family from the grief his has felt,
he thinks his brother would be proud of him.
that's all he wants: to help people
like the ones he wished he could have saved.
they wish him good luck, and he hopes it's enough.
he hopes he is enough.

in nine years, Peter will be twenty-three.
a year older than his older brother,
and he'll find himself back at this school,
he will have written several full-length books.
some children's, explaining grief; a poetry book he's avoided working on
due to it being his brother's passion that he quit before he got bad again.

he is here not for himself, but Alex's stepdaughter will be the one on stage.
and she will not know death close to home
until after she's halfway through high school.

Peter did end the cycle, but it wasn't easy,
however, Alex was always there for him.
he felt like an older brother, and he wasn't Neil, but Peter knew
if Neil wanted him to have anyone else, it would have been him.
he would be proud of both if he could see them now.

Alex won't see his stepdaughter graduate, but Peter will.
and in the very opening page of the book, it'll read,
"Dedicated to Alexis Neal".

leave the light on, when you go

the day after your older sibling dies

the morning after your older sibling dies,
you will wake like any other morning.
they will not be there, but you can still faintly hear the door creak open
as you went to tell them of a nightmare, you had the night before.
years ago, when your hero was still your friend, before they got meaner.
the mourning birds will sing the same, and your morning is still a fresh start,
for a minute or two it feels like you're back home, in some sweet spring air,
before everything, when things are still okay.

you think things will always be this way forever,
and even though you know it won't, you still hope.
until you open your phone, the missed calls feel like a sharp cut to your heart.
when you call back the voice on the other side is tender, whether it's your
mother, father, sister, brother, or a nurse who reads off their name on a chart,
and ends their message with condolences, the same ones you'll hear
a thousand times after, the words will start to lose their meaning.

you'll never get back the life you had before they were gone.
you'll envy other people, who can just say, "I'm sorry"
and not have to see the loss in every part of your life.
in your reflection, it feels like some part of you's missing.
the only other person who lived a life like yours at the start,
you'll never see them grow up past the age they were.
your only way of seeing them again will be through photographs
and old videos, all the old memories with them will be the only ones
you'll ever get to have with them.

the day after your older sibling dies, you'll blame yourself.
you know that isn't wasn't your fault,
but guilt doesn't care who's to blame,
it'll affect any heart at a loss.

you'll try to be strong, like the example they were for you but on your own,
you think you're weaker than them, but don't worry, they won't have to know.
you'll watch your family change, the gatherings become smaller,
and you will think about their dreams, what and who they wanted to be when
they grew up, they will never get to have that.
you will try to forgive them for being mean as a teenager,
you will remember the things they had done for you,
the times they ignored you when you asked to play because now you can't
hear their side, you can't get closure from them, your memories of them are
the only part of them you will be able to keep.

whether you believe in religion or not, you'll feel lost
and you can only hope they aren't anymore.
the hours will drag on for days, and the weeks will pass so fast,
that you won't realize it's already been two months without them.
you can't seem to catch up with everyone else,
who had them only as a friend of a year, or a month,
a cousin, who only spoke to them at Christmas.
a life without them is something you never thought you'd have to see,
but now you have to live every day of it.

you'd trade yourself for them if you could, but no amount of wanting
and wishing can bring them back in any living form.
all the people they could have met will never know
what it's like to have them in their lives.
you'll think of them back when they were your age
and wish you could have just another minute
with them, and ask them what you should do next,
but you will never be able to ask them for their thoughts or advice again.

you think you were never supposed to be older than them
but someday you would be eventually,
and you could live with that but now feels too soon.
you'll hear over and over *it'll get easier*, but it doesn't feel like it ever will.
you'll replay the old videos and stare at old photos,
there will never be a new one with them taken.
someday you'll look into the mirror, and see a version of them,
they'll never live to be.

you'll see them everywhere, in the kids with bright hopeful eyes,
and the teenagers with scars.

when important life events happen,
they won't be there to celebrate or mourn with you,
every video you send will never be seen, you'll never be left on read again,
but the text will someday turn to green, and someone might text back,
but it'll be a question you'll never know about them again, *"who are you?"*

six months after your older sibling dies,
you'll go out and for the first time in a while,
you'll feel like you can breathe again.
you'll still see them in people with familiar faces but none of them will
recognize you.

star hands

every time you come across a photo from the year before,
something they liked before they were gone, or something that described
the both of you so perfectly well, your heart will sink when you remember,
their name will never come up on your screen again.

your family's faces will always be stuck in your mind,
the funeral was the last time you'd ever gather somewhere for them.
you'll miss the little things, the things you used to get annoyed at them for,
but also all the milestones you'll never see them reach,
the ones they won't see you reach either.

you'll never see who they could have become,
they will never see who you will end up being.
you've thought over and over what you could've done,
what you could have said, but there isn't anything you can do,
it's already happened, and you can't go back to save them.
you feel like it's your fault regardless like you could've prevented it
in some way, but you couldn't and can't.
you wish you spent more time with them while you could,
but there is no amount of time you could ever spend
with the dead that would be enough to erase the wish for just another day.

a year after your older sibling dies, their birthday will have come and passed,
a year after your older sibling dies, your birthday will have come and passed.
you'll think about them, as you knew them a few years ago,
and try to imagine who they would have become.
they were older than you then,
but you're now older than they'll ever get to be.
you've thought over and over, of what you could say,
a thousand times it has happened in your mind.

they have died, and there is nothing you can do about it,
yet you feel it is your fault.
it isn't, it is not your fault.
it isn't your fault, no matter how many nights you lay awake
trying to convince yourself there is something you could have done.
it isn't, and wasn't your fault.

leave the light on, when you go

bastard son of the drunken sun

bastard son, of the drunken sun, lay low on cold nights.
with your hands still cold from the beer,
no matter how numb your fingers are,
you'll never numb the feeling of loneliness.
when you crawl into your bed quietly,
you'll remember you will wake no one even if you scream your lungs out.
you'll call your mother's number, but remember she changed it last July
and you won't remember anyone else's but your own.
it seems like your childhood was worse than you remember
when you see yourself in the mirror.
but you'll never go back, you'll never go back,
how are you going to live with that?
with your heart that loves like poison, and your hands that can't be warmed
by another's, you always pull away before they find out how you got here.
aren't you lonely, being your father's son?
is it shameful to hate yourself when you see him in your own eyes
when your mother loved him enough to forgive him
for mistakes he didn't believe in?
you won't know, but now you will rest in the same fate
your mother was afraid of, but at least you kissed her goodbye
the last time you saw her.
at least you know even if god doesn't forgive you, your mother will.
you always wondered how she did it, how could she forgive him for what he
became, what he did to her and you.
she'd probably say something about how it was all worth it
because you're her baby—she wouldn't have you without him.
but you feel ridden with sin you can't be clean of.
instead of the gentle warmth, her voice wrapped you in
when his anger festered like bees in a knocked-down hive.
convinced the structure of your house was too weak to handle his heavy
shoulders, you swore you'd have a quiet house.
it's what you lived for, a fantasy just barely out of your reach.
you wondered what dreams meant now that you were let down from his
shoulders, the closest you'd ever be to the moon.
now your mother's hands tremble when they hold yours.
you are sure that if there is an afterlife, she will be there to hold your hand,
and maybe there, your father will hold your hand as tightly as the bottle,
when you stumble trying to get used to clouds beneath,
like a baby taking their first steps,
maybe this time he will be around to see you grow.

leave the light on, when you go

the blue house, and the family of ghosts

it is summertime, and the neighborhood kids are riding their bikes.
Christian and I are sitting out on the porch.
we talk about the things the adults wouldn't tell us before.
but we're older now; I turn sixteen soon, him seventeen.
he bites at his lip, and I do my cheek.
I keep my hands in my pockets, flicking a broken lighter on and off.
he picks at the skin on his thumb as he watches
his younger brother play with the dog.

I break the silence.
"did you know that boy, the one who lives in the blue house?"
it sits across from where we are.
there is a white picket fence and a gorgeous garden right up against the house.

"the one who shot himself?" Christian's eyes are focused ahead.

"yeah. do you know why he did it?"
I ask and turn my head in the same direction as his.

"no, but I wish I did. maybe then, I could've…I don't know,
saved him if I knew what to look for," he says, almost as if he'll get closure.

"were you friends?"

"no, but I saw him around, I wonder if we had been, if I could have done
something."

"yeah, I get that, but you didn't, and you couldn't have."

Christian's brother plays fetch with the dog while a cat walks along the trash
cans outside the blue house, and a man walks out to get the newspaper.
the dead boy's sister—the man's daughter—comes to take out the trash.

we watch as the cat jumps down,
and she clicks her tongue, calling it to follow her inside.
we catch her gaze for a second, and then she turns away,
none of us say anything. any time we see her, or any time we saw him
because we don't know them, but we wish that we had because now, we can't.

leave the light on, when you go

we're too scared of saying the wrong thing, I think.
we always think there's next time until there's never a time again.
the son was too scared to reach for help
because he had thought he was already too far gone.
the daughter would rather feel nothing than to have to admit the absence,
but it'll wash her over, pull her under until she recognizes she's drowning.
her father drowns himself in anything that'll go down
because blacking out seems a better option
than to see the sun come up in a world without his son.
their mother can barely utter the word daughter, before breaking down
knowing she used to be a mother to two
instead of one shell of a child, and a ghost,
who she feels dying again and again every morning she wakes.

things they don't tell you about growing up ugly

I'm funny, but not funny enough to laugh with at three a.m.
I am someone you look forward to seeing,
but never remember after you leave.
I am good at poetry, but I'm better at writing endings
than I am at starting new beginnings.
I'm pretty, but not confession-worthy.
beautiful, but I've never been told so by anyone outside my family.
you want to hold my hand in winter,
but I want affection from more than a friendship.
a friend of mine said everyone will eventually find their person.
I didn't remind her that the only chance I had of getting married was to her
if she still didn't have anyone else by our late thirties.
she met her boyfriend two weeks after that,
and we stopped being friends at some point after,
neither of us can quite remember.
I am by no means bitter, and I am happy she is not alone.
I just hope that I get to have that same connection with another person.

people like you if you're quiet, or if you're loud, as long as you're pretty.
it's quirky to be weird if you're still appealing on the outside.
it's cute if you're awkward; you're allowed to have a few flaws
if your smile is nice enough.
I watch as the years go by, and as more and more
of my friends find no issue in finding their people,
I'm starting to wonder if maybe there's just something wrong with me.

she said, "give them time—someday when you're older, they'll see your
beauty." but I think if people have to mature and grow up
to see me as beautiful, then I don't think I ever was.
every time I've ever said I felt like I was ugly, I was met with compliments
about how I was a great listener, funny, and a great friend,
instead of all the ways I was wrong.

people used to dare their friends to ask me out.
they'd joke about dating me as if it was a disgusting nightmare
that anyone would dream of the day they could wake from,
even when I had hardly even said hello to them.
but when someone had done it to a girl that most people liked,
it was seen as wrong—even to the people who she had talked about
behind their backs, stood up for her.

leave the light on, when you go

everyone I have dated preferred personality over looks,
and was already my best friend before they ever thought about being with me.
I know being used for your body isn't a good thing but for once,
I'd like for someone to love me for the part of me I've been taught to hide,
the part of me I've had to make up for, with my personality,
in my every word.
I want someone to finally see me as art before they do a poet.

I will watch all of my friends fall in love over and over again.
and I will stare at my hands and look up at the sky,
and ask god what is wrong with him to give me such a heart
that could be more than enough,
in a body that is too hard to look at to be able to love.

star hands

worthy

I'm running my hands through my hair asking, "is it that hard to love me?"
my hair is soft, I am soft.
I give so much love. it is messy, yes, but it is love, my love.
why do I receive nothing in return when I give my all?
you can braid aspects of our personalities together
until I'm something worth fighting for.

my nails are painted, and chipped, but worthy of being held, right?
I keep everything given to me in separate boxes,
so, the memories and nightmares don't touch each other.
so, I can believe your love for me was genuine
and the heartache was a cost for something else.

I don't know if I'm worthy of it, but I want it
I want it like it's all I've been made to do,
a hunger for which there is no other cure.
self-love can only do so much—no matter how hard I close my eyes,
I cannot love myself like someone else can,
like someone who can walk away but chooses to stay.

I am sentimental, and I want to be beautiful entirely to somebody.
is it too much for me to ask to be looked at
and not turned away from at sight of my flaws?
when I can't feel whole, when I need you most, I want you to stay.

I swear to you, my hands are just bruised and calloused;
I know they are ugly, but they can be beautiful, just give me a chance.
let me love you, let me be worthy of somebody,
show me somebody worth me.

pride

we sit on top of the hill, and he asks me, "if we are still together
when we're old enough to be, will we even be able to get married?"

I reassure him that we'll figure out something if we can't, we don't have to be
for this to be real: if we are still together then, we could just live together if
that's all we can do.

"but it isn't fair, we could just get this taken from us," he says.

"it's not our fault we're the same gender.
we didn't choose this, we chose each other."

he asks me, "how is this different than if we were a boy and girl?"

I hold his hand. "it's not, but I doubt it'll come to that."
he sighs. "yeah, you're probably right."

and when we walk out in the city, I hold his hand tighter
when we pass some guy on a corner with a sign
with an umbrella over a family with a rainbow falling.

when we pass by another queer couple, we exchange a glance, and a soft
smile. it is a relief to know there are people like you, even when people
pretend there aren't.

LGBTQ+ people have always been here, for as long as everyone else,
we're all human.

nobody should have to live in fear because of who they love, who they are,
and someday, I hope this fear of death for pride will cease.
I hope we will not have to die to be heard any longer.

I know it is not as bad as it was once, but I know people whose families
would rather disown them than have a gay daughter or a trans son.

I know it is not as bad as it used to be, but I can count how many years
it's been since gay marriage was legalized on two hands.

I know it is not as bad as it once was but there are still people being treated as
they had been before.

I know it is not as bad as it once was, but we still can improve.

star hands

I know it is not as bad as it once was,
but sometimes I fear someday it might be.

leave the light on, when you go

hummingbird

puffy eyes, and soundless pleas for something more than this.
it's ironic to be told you are saving lives while you sit losing yours.
I am being told I'm so mature for my age,
while I am afraid, I am of growing into an immature adult
in attempt to relive a past I never should have known.
a beautiful poem in exchange for a week's worth of sleeping through the day,
words lined up that perfectly describe the feeling I can't name.
if I could, I'd give up my art for peace of mind,
one quiet night to stop feeling like a ghost.
but when it's just us, I get a feeling like this will never end,
and it always does, no matter how long it lasts.
when I'm with you, I feel more like art than a person.

leave the light on, when you go

remember when/I do

my house will be built on the foundation of sunlight's embrace.
gentle brushes across skin like petals to fingertips with thin enough curtains
that the early morning washes us over like cold water.
when you come home, I'll be waiting for you.
early evening or late night, I'll kiss you goodnight.
we can sit on the porch in the early mornings
before we go to the store on the weekend.
I can tell you of the things I've made since the last time you asked,
and you can tell me all the stories you've brought to life.
I'll buy you flowers at the end of every week when they restock.
I'll attend your every show and be the biggest fan in the front row.
if money runs short, we'll have a garden to pick from, I'm sure.
I know you'll convince me to follow what I dream, even though I'm nervous.
you'll say you'll be there every step, and we'll mess around in the kitchen,
drunk on laughter like we did when we were teenagers,
slow dancing as if we ever knew how to, and in our bedroom,
we'll whisper, maybe we're getting better, then fall onto the bed.

the house will be quiet when we go to bed,
but in the day, we'll be quick to fill it with music.
you can sit on the counter while I try to decipher the recipe,
and you'll remind me that my contacts are on the bedside table.
they'll ask us when it started, and it'll be hard to remember life before you.
even when I didn't know you, I knew I was waiting for someone like you.
and when the fireworks go off,
when the storm gets closer, I'll hold your hand.
I'll remind you I'm there every night
you start to think you might be on your own,
I'll always be here for you.

in the sunset, we will kiss in front of the open window,
without a care about who sees us.
someone someday will ask me how I know I love you,
and I'll say I know because I can't imagine a world
where I write a poem about love and am not talking about you;
even in poems about loving life, I still find you in at least a sentence or two.

leave the light on, when you go

every Christmas will be like the ones when we were kids,
magical and special.

we'll watch every romance movie on the list of all the best
and accidentally burn the sugar cookies.

I'll make hot chocolate, mine doused in peppermint
and yours with none but full of whipped cream.

the living things we bring into our home will never see us fight,
we'll make them embarrassed to be seen with us.

I'll do the things you wrote are must-dos on your list from the fairytales.
I will wash your hair, and you will paint my nails;
I will cook and you will sweep.
you'll take your coffee cold and I'll take my tea hot
on the nights we have more to do.
in the summertime, we'll hold hands in our sleep,
and the cats will curl up at our feet.
I will make my life something to find comfort in.
I will live long enough to have somewhere to call home,
on my own, or with you by my side as I'd much rather.
it'll be not so far soon someday,
and I'll miss my youth but if I'm free to love you,
then I'll settle for my "remember when?" having an "I do."

how to get over your ex

1. don't go to that place just because you might see them there,
   go there because they have your favorite thing, a food or drink,
   a certain bouquet. don't check your phone for messages you know
   aren't coming, you'll only hurt your feelings.

2. accept the time spent—love is never a waste
   just because it wasn't forever.

3. know you were whole before and after they came into your life.
   you will feel that happiness you did with them again, on your own
   someday, or someone else further down the line. no matter how long
   it takes you to heal, you'll be okay.

4. see them for what they are: not as who you love,
   but rather as their actions, how they made you feel,
   what it was, not what it could have been.

5. do you want them back, or are you just scared of being alone?
   if you don't know, you have to ask yourself,
   and listen to nobody but yourself for this answer.
   did you like yourself when you were with them?
   how did they make you feel?

6. know that it's not your fault if you had someone who didn't love you
   in the way you should have been.
   we can learn to accept love that we deserve more
   than what we've gotten.
   you are not broken, although your heart may feel like it might be.
   you will love again.

7. know the memories, but don't spend hours looking at them.
   look at your smile and think of how someday
   sooner than you think you'll feel that again,
   love comes around full circle—there is no complete end.

8. you do not have to have closure from the other person to move on.
   I'd argue it makes it harder.
   you ask one question and suddenly you're an investigator,
   you never want to have any of your questions unanswered again.
   you'll wonder what one thing had meant, but it means nothing now,
   there's no use dwelling on the past now that you've decided to look
   ahead. you can miss them, but you do not have to tell them.

9. you can cry, you can miss them, and you can want them back
    and still understand it wasn't right.
    you can feel nothing and it doesn't mean the love wasn't there.
    you can deal with it however you'd like,
    but if it's meant to happen it will find its way,
    and it may be on some better day that you two meet
    and find reconnection.
    maybe after some time spent with friends again,
    or after several long months of being strangers,
    but you cannot live your life on a string of hope.
    you need to live for yourself, you cannot live with someone else
    healthily if you cannot live your life for yourself first.

10. know that you will be okay,
    however it plays out, however long it's been.
    you will be loved, and the memories will still be there
    to look back on, that version of you,
    who you were when you were in love isn't lost.
    you just need to find something else now to bring it back.
    do something that makes you happy, alone or with a friend
    or family member, and watch as the nights pass easier,
    and the sunrise comes in gentler like a kiss on the cheek.
    there is love all around you and has always been
    because like the earth you grow each day, you are full of love
    from everything you've ever been a part of;
    someone's only recollection of you is a smiling you,
    when you passed them by on the street, or someplace,
    you were too caught up in your mind to notice
    your eyes had that spark in them again.
    which is proof that part of you is not gone forever.

11. do not fill the void with other people.
    not only will you potentially hurt them, but you will hurt yourself.
    rebounds do not bring you back into the game,
    just tangle you in a mess of strings
    you'd be much better without ever touching.
    casual love is fine, but don't use people to fill what they can't
    and would never be able to without them knowing.

12. do not rewatch the same romantic movies
    if they make you cry until you throw up; they won't help.
    instead, call your friend and watch a thriller together,
    talk about how the popcorn is a little too salty and how the actor
    has starred in all your favorite movies since you were ten.

13. see every day as a new start.
    don't expect it to be easy, but don't hold yourself back
    from making it better than the last, because someday you'll look back
    nearly a year later and you'll be entirely different.

14. talk about it, write about it, make art about it—whatever you do,
    have an outlet. bottling it up won't make it go away.
    talk about the bad, and the good, to those you trust to not give you
    biased opinions, those who will just listen
    instead of telling you what it meant, and what to think.

    it doesn't have to be to a real person—you can write down
    and close the book, let the weight of the words find their place
    on the lines instead of your chest.

    pretend for a moment, you can transfer the feeling completely
    into paper, though I know it doesn't work like that,
    it can ease the burden; it is worth a try at least.

15. know you will come out of this.
    you will not be like how you used to be,
    what that means for you depends on what you want it to,
    but you cannot go back to how things used to be,
    because that version of you then,
    will always become this version of you.

16. remember that just as there were reasons that it happened,
    there are reasons it ended.
    reflect on what happened, otherwise,
    you'll likely end up in the same situation as before.
    rarely things are one person's fault.
    sometimes it's a pure inconvenience,
    both parties or something neither of you can't fix.
    putting blame on someone or accusing won't bring them back,
    but you can work on yourself and improve your behavior so your
    next relationship may have fewer problems before it even starts.
    you will have to work on yourself eventually.

17. you can never go back to the past; beyond the memories you keep.
    that is all of you and them that will ever exist, for now.
    and if it does happen to be that you find your way back to each other,
    it probably won't happen when you expect it to, if at all,
    you'll have to relearn who they have become since you've been apart.

18. they'll change, and so will you, embrace it,
    because even without you noticing, you'll forget the habits
    you picked up from them, and they'll pick up someone else's.

    holding onto a pure wish won't get you anywhere,
    except stuck in the idea of a life you will never have.
    eventually and undoubtedly, you will be pulled back to the ground,
    whether you come to realize it sooner or later,
    the hurt will turn to resentment if you don't let go.

star hands

the bear or man question

the man will walk free even if I scream.
the bear would be euthanized if it was seen.
you will be believed if you say a bear attacked you,
they'll defend you with, "It's simply in their nature."
but monster could never be their baby boy, their son.
they'd say they raised him well,
so it must be your fault; "what were *you* wearing?"
ignoring the fact you're someone's baby too,
and ignoring infants and soldiers have been victims, too.
every time you get suspicious,
they'll say not all men; they're one out of thousands.

but one out of three women have been sexually assaulted in the United States
in their lifetime, one out of thirty men have been sexually assaulted
and around ninety percent of preparators are men.

I've never encountered a bear, but I knew some rapists
by their names before their crimes.

there's never enough time

star hands

things they don't tell you when your mom dies

you will feel sixteen and angry, four and lost in the grocery store.
your first home will be gone, and the person who loved you into existence
isn't going to call you or wipe away your tears or tuck you into bed
on restless nights when the dreams are the only memories,
you can keep unstained by reality.
you'll search for words to explain every detail of her life and fail, knowing
she'll never be more than mom to you; you think that if you met her
as a young woman, or as a child, you may have been friends,
or family from another lifetime.
you could find more to say of her life before you,
find some way to give her some sympathy
without having to break a part of your heart but she raised you,
and you cannot forgive her for it no matter how hard you try.
some part of you blames yourself for the way she was.
some part of you blames her for the way you are.
you didn't have a key to the house, but you lived there, nonetheless.
the words tremble on top of your tongue, sinking into your teeth
like the first bite you took from fruit.
when speaking of the person who taught you to speak,
her story will feel like one of a stranger, but it's only yours to tell now.
when they ask you who raised you, you'll hesitate. who was she?
the woman who washed the dirt off your body
or the woman who caused the scars on your skin?
were they separate or one?
your mother, the woman who loved you more than anyone,
who in your eyes was the most beautiful person to walk;
the woman who tore apart your view of your body
before you ever even realized you were looking at a mirror.
the one who defended your name and used it against you,
in between the fights and days that you knew she loved you.
you'll never know what was from love and how empty her threats were.
you are your mother's child and will be to the day you die.
you die the day your mother does, and there is nothing you can do to go back
home. you turn on the light, but there's nobody to check for monsters,
or let you into their room for a night or two.
when her screams linger,
when her voice is the only voice that could put you to sleep,
there'll be no denying the weight you carry as an absence of a hand to hold.

the day after your younger sibling dies

the morning after your younger sibling dies,
you will wake like any other morning.
they will not be there, but you could still faintly hear
one of their retellings of a nightmare they had the night before,
years ago when they were younger before you got meaner.

the mourning birds will sing the same, and your morning is still a fresh start.
for a minute or two it feels like you're back home, in some sweet spring air,
you hope things will always be this way forever,
and even though you know they won't.
you open your phone, and the missed calls feel like a sharp cut to your heart.

the voice on the other side is tender,
whether it's your mother, father, sister, brother, or a nurse
who reads off their name on a chart,
and ends their message with condolences,
the same ones you'll hear a thousand times after;
the words will start to lose their meaning.
you'll never get back the life you had before they were gone.
you'll envy other people who can just say, "I'm sorry"
and not have to see the loss in every part of your life.
in your reflection, it feels like some part of you's missing.
the only other person who lived a life like yours at the start,
you'll never see them grow up past the age they were.

your only way of seeing them again will be through photographs
and old videos, all the old memories with them
will be the only ones you'll ever get to have with them.
the day after your younger sibling dies, you'll blame yourself.
you know that isn't wasn't your fault, but guilt doesn't care who's to blame,
it'll affect any heart.

you'll try to be strong, like the example you had to be for them.
but on your own, you think you're weaker than them.
don't worry, they won't have to know.
you'll watch your family change. the gatherings become smaller.
people will slip up and ask where they are, and you'll have to repeat the
news, until it's harder to remember a time
when they were still there in the family photos.

you will think about their dreams, what and who
they wanted to be when they grew up.

star hands

you'll miss the little kid who always asked you to play with them
and forget they were older than you were when they were born.
whether you believe in religion or not, you'll feel lost
and you can only hope they aren't anymore.
the hours will drag on for days, and the weeks will pass so fast.
that you won't realize it's already been two months without them.
you can't seem to catch up with everyone else, who had them only as a friend
of a year, or a month, or a cousin who only spoke to them at Christmas.
a life without them is something you never thought you'd have to see,
but now you have to live every day of it.

you'd trade yourself for them if you could, but no amount of wanting
and wishing can bring them back in any living form.
all the people they could have met will never know
what it's like to have them in their lives.
you will never know what it is like to see them at the age you are now.

you were always going to be older than them for as long as you were here,
but someday they were supposed to be older than you,
and you could live with that.
but the gap between you two was never supposed to be bigger
than it was when they were born.

you'll hear over and over that it'll get easier,
but it doesn't feel like it ever will.
you'll replay the old videos and stare at old photos,
trying to memorize their features, so maybe you can look into the mirror
and see a version of them, they'll never live to be.

you'll see them everywhere, in the little kids with bright hopeful eyes,
and the teenagers with scars. when important life events happen,
they won't be there to celebrate or mourn with you.

every video you send will never be seen, you'll never be left on read again,
but the text will someday turn to green, and someone might text back,
"who are you?"

six months after your younger sibling dies, you'll go out,
and for the first time in a while, you'll feel like you can breathe again.
you'll still see them in people with familiar faces but none of them will
recognize you.

every time you come across a post they liked or a memory from years ago,
something that described the both of you so perfectly well,
your heart will sink when you remember,
their name will never come up on your screen again.

your family's faces will always be stuck in your mind.
the funeral was the last time you'd ever gather somewhere for them.
you'll miss the little things, the things you used to get annoyed at them for,
but also all the milestones you'll never see them reach,
the ones they won't see you reach either.

you'll never see who they could have become,
they will never see who you will end up being.
you've thought over and over what you could've done,
what you could have said, but there isn't anything you can do,
it's already happened, and you can't go back to save them.

you feel like it's your fault regardless like you should've changed sooner,
spent more time with them while you could,
but there is no amount of time you could ever spend with the dead
that would be enough to erase the wish for just another day.

a year after your younger sibling dies,
their birthday will have come and passed,
a year after your younger sibling dies,
your birthday will have come and passed.
you'll think about them, as you knew them a year ago,
and try to imagine who they would have become.
they were younger than you, but you're now older than they'll ever get to be.
you've thought over and over, of what you could say,
a thousand times it has happened in your mind.
they have died, and there is nothing you can do about it,
yet you feel it is your fault.

it isn't, it is not your fault.
it isn't your fault, no matter how many nights you lay awake
trying to convince yourself there is something you could have done.
it isn't and wasn't your fault.

what to do on the last week of school

Monday. don't dread the start of the week.
think of how you'll never be here again like how you are now in four days.
you never liked counting the day you're living in
because the years leading up to now felt like a lifetime away.
now you'd do anything for another hour with your friends, and family.
hug all of your friends.
even if you aren't a big hug person, maybe this time accept the offer.
who knows if you'll ever cross paths again besides the occasional,
"how are you doing?" message around the holidays, or a happy birthday
or two before it's someone else's special day?
you may never even pass each other when you come back home
for Christmas or summer, this might be your last chance
to say anything at all that you've promised to say next time.

as you leave your final class,
you look at your younger friends you're leaving behind.
you won't be here anymore to help them look forward to the future,
or stick around as the proof it gets better,
someday they'll be what you were to them for someone else,
and then the cycle will repeat.

Tuesday. draw a picture with the sun in the corner
before you leave for school, with you and your family,
your friends, and your pet(s).
write on the back who you want to be when you're twenty-five.
keep it somewhere you know you won't lose it.
bring a notebook and let your friends draw in it, write something.
signing yearbooks is an option, but you can do more with a bigger space.
someone might write a thing or two about you that you never noticed
before, or a memory long forgotten.
if you don't have anyone to share the moment with, write letters to yourself.
ask future you how they're doing, ask about that one thing,
make one wish in each for them.
store them in the same place as you did your drawing.
you've waited years for this week, and now
you've got something to look forward to and back on again.

Wednesday. hold your breath for a few seconds.
breathe in and out and recognize the beat of your heart.
know that whatever happens, for now, you are alive, you have made it.

through every moment you were convinced you wouldn't,
cordless or not—the fact you get to wear the gown is a pride
that not every person gets to have

Thursday. find old friendship bracelets, letters, photos,
and dream of this day like it's still six years away like you've still got hope
that your friends and you are forever.
propose the idea of making new ones with your friends
to show how much things have changed.
go outside, listen, watch, sit on the lawn, and think about what little you
would ask if they could ask about anything at all,
whose name would they mention first, after your own?
ask yourself who you'd ask older you about now.
take a picture of yourself, even if you don't look your best.
future you will hold it close to your heart like a parent to baby pictures.
you're still so young, you're still learning and growing,
and you have your whole life ahead of you.
enjoy this moment while it lasts.

Friday, you used to wait all week for Friday.
as you got older it meant temporary relief,
maybe not fully but another thing off your plate.
now this Friday is a real end—not to your life,
but the one that you spent so long waiting to grow out of.
when you walk through your elementary school,
you'll feel just like the scared five-year-olds who will hide
behind their mother's knees come august.
the newest teachers are less than half your age now,
yet you feel like you're still learning how to spell your name,
just trying to figure out who you are.
you don't know what you want to be
for the rest of your life right now, but you don't have to.
you can figure it out—you will figure it out.

you will sometimes never outgrow a version of little you,
hold their hand, and walk into the new phase,
show them what the future holds, and make a life
you'd be proud to show younger you.

love and lose: it is only normal. heal and accept, give yourself mercy,
and give it to those around you— it is all our first time living.
but know, that not everyone's meant to stay,
and a reason doesn't equal excuse.

a life is not rich with only one kind of experience.
have an open mind and embrace change with open arms.
step out of your comfort zone to find what is and what is not for you.
do not be afraid to make mistakes, or to say no.
live a life, that makes death something to fear.

leave the light on, when you go

the day after your friend dies

the day your friend dies, you will wake up, they will not.
the day after your friend dies, you will turn on your phone
and see new messages, but none from them.
you'll think about their family, their pets,
cousins, siblings, but mostly think about them.
you'll wonder what they said when their eyes closed,
and pray it's something as gentle as they were.
you will wander through the day, feeling stuck in an endless loop
trying to make sense of the signs they've left behind.
you'll get condolences, but none of them
will ever comfort you like they could.
you will hear over and over again: *it gets easier.*
but the fear of forgetting makes you scared for it to be.
you'll see their favorite things, a movie franchise,
a kind of flower, a certain holiday, and miss the spark that lit in their eyes
when they spoke about it, you'll miss the way they'd talk.
you'll replay their voicemails and videos until you can't bear to.
sometime later you'll swipe down too far on social media,
and see a post they liked at some point,
and suddenly it's as if you've just heard the news.
you'll see a video, or a photo, a thing you're rushing to tell them,
and as you press send, the text changes to green instead of seen.

six months after your friend dies, you'll go out, and for the first time, you
won't see them in everything. some things, sure, but it'll hurt you a little less
every day you will try so hard to not forget, but you lose small parts of the
memories every time you try to remember it all so clearly.
people will laugh and smile, talk
and carry themselves tall in the crowd when you pass by.
you'll watch the world move on without them,
but always feel their ghost's presence.
you'll think about what you could've done to save them,
but it wasn't your fault.

things would always turn out this way;
everyone would always make these decisions.
after all, none of us knew the consequences of our actions
before we took them.

you will often think about the funeral and the distress on their family's faces.
you will maintain contact with maybe their mother, and for a while,
it will feel like you have some half of them still by your side.

star hands

a year after your friend passes, their birthday will have come and passed.
a year after your friend passes, your birthday will have came and passed.
you will think about them, as you knew them a year ago,
and try to imagine who they would have become.
they were older than you then, but now you're older
than they'll ever get to be.
you'll miss the little things, but also all the milestones they'll never reach.
you'll miss seeing who they could have become,
and they'll never see who you will become.
you've thought over and over, of what you could've said,
a thousand times it has happened in your mind.
they have died, and there is nothing you can do about it,
yet you feel it is your fault.
it isn't, it is not your fault.
it isn't your fault, no matter how many nights you lay awake
trying to convince yourself there is something you could have done.
it isn't, and wasn't your fault.

leave the light on, when you go

changing by staying the same

I'm cleaning out my closet. posters hung once by newly bought tape
have already fallen apart, though it's barely been a year.
pacing around my room, I memorize the way the ceiling looks so low now.
when I was younger, I was afraid to make my room mine,
I was afraid I would change, but now in every corner,
a part of me shines like a star out in space.
I watch every box fill itself.

I'm standing in the middle of the driveaway.
we used to chase each other all around here.
I lived only three blocks from my best friends
when I was in fourth grade, but now there is nothing left here for me.
I grew up here, and I'll grow up somewhere else; it never felt like home here.
I swear I heard ghosts crying in the walls.

when we drove here behind the trucks I had braids in my hair.
I was terrified of change, because if things changed,
how was I going to stay the same?
but when we arrived, we unboxed every item as carefully as it was boxed.
I told my old friends I was convinced this house was haunted.
now, I am the ghost that will haunt someone else's house.
fights and makeup that hold up the walls of my childhood house,
glitter glue and scratch and sniff stickers found
four years after its last been used, names that'll never be spoken again
meaning the same person here, the house I had my first kiss
in may very well be where someone has their last.

I pull out of the driveway, my hair dyed by a friend, and I have changed.
I am constantly changing even by staying the same, I am never not,
and for as long as I am alive, I grow and I change,
staying the same day by day, but by the end of the year,
it's hard to recognize myself in a photo from January every year.

letters I couldn't send to anyone

fell in love

two years ago, I fell in love with a girl
who knew the worst parts of me all too well,
and not enough of the gentler parts of me I was still trying to grow.
we weren't right for each other,
but there isn't a day I don't hope she finds peace.

three years ago, I fell in love with the person I will become.
I looked in the mirror and for the first time, I believed more that someday,
I would wake up proud one day that I made it,
and than I believed I wouldn't make it another year.

four years ago, I fell in love with myself, and the way that I am.
I did not make peace with it yet, but I let it be this way
and didn't try to hide it now.

five years ago, I fell in love with the stars
and the way that they were so far away
but never took that as a reason to not shine their light on us.
the moon is the same anywhere, but the stars
above my hometown are a part of the past—
I can never see them again with my naked eyes.

six years ago, I fell in love with the sun and the way it kissed my skin to tan.

six years ago, I fell in love with the bugs and the things
I would now turn from.
I fell in love with the ugly, and I found beauty in anything that came near me.

six years ago, I fell in love with myself in the mirror,
when I didn't have expectations for how I was supposed to look like yet.

seven years ago, I fell in love with summer,
the hot weather that brushed off the winter breeze
like dust that had collected on a book.
spring couldn't wait to turn the next page it read too quickly,
and now august was here.
a new school year began. I still felt as small as the year before,
but I wore shoes two sizes bigger than I did last fall.

eight years ago, I fell in love with writing,
before I had ever done it on my own, I fell in love with characters,
and people whose imaginations were worlds of fantasy.
I fell in love with poetry before I ever memorized a poem,
I knew that someday that's what I wanted to create.

nine years ago, I fell in love with art,
in a small corner by the sun, I named myself the artist.
I recreated art the only way I knew it, summertime in my backyard.
my parents hung the drawing on the fridge,
it stayed there for years until I got embarrassed by it.

a year ago, I fell in love with who I am becoming,
my art, my passion, the way that I look again,
and how well certain clothes compliment my features.
I fell in love with my family and friends,
how we are all bound by a connection of love,
and admiration for one another, how none of us would be here
if someone didn't love someone.
I fell in love with the good and bad of my life.
I felt grateful I could experience any of this.
how small were the chances that my friends I would have met?
how small were the chances that I'd be me?
how small were the chances that you and I would cross paths?

we don't know how long anything lasts.

so, take a minute to recognize you are here
because someone loved someone because stars exist,
you will not have forever for anything.

leave the light on, when you go

how to never stop being sad

1. every time you see something bad, let it linger and fester inside of you.
feel its coldness and watch as the people around you laugh and smile.

2. find comfort in it. spend so much time-consuming media and revisiting
thoughts that encourage it until it's second nature, your new normal.
every time you talk to someone, speak negatively to the point it is impossible
for someone to have a conversation with you without feeling drained. but you
already believe that this is what you make people feel like, don't you?

3. slip away even as you stand there: be somewhere else, a walking ghost.
become everything you've ever hated,
because now this is all you've ever wanted.
lose interest in your passions.
become dull and tired for a sleep that you can only reach alone.

4. listen to sad music on repeat. let the lyrics embody your life.
when someone asks if you are doing okay, push them away.
get angry: *how dare they stop you? how dare they care now?*
repeat yourself it is too late.
not even you can save yourself now.

5. write, over and over, the reasons you are unlovable.
write all the reasons you think your friends hate you, surely now,
they must do if you have any left that is.
write until your head hurts, until you're too tired to pick up a pen.

6. don't get up from your bed, until you can't on your own.
neglect all basic hygiene, become a carcass in your room,
and watch the mold grow and the trash build up.
let it become a mirror of yourself, and believe this is who you are.

7. repeat the memories you used to try to distract yourself from.
there's no use in the distractions if you want this feeling, talk to it,
hear its whisper, and watch as it becomes a scream, a plea.
you want to be seen but you cannot take the help
no matter how badly you know you need it.
you can't admit it, in fear of being seen as weak; in fear of burdening others,
you abandon your self-worth.

8. watch the days turn into months since you've left your house.
lose your life while you're still alive and wonder how
you'll ever make it in "the real world."

9. start writing again, this time the letters.
put careful detail into every why—there will be many questions,
but so few answers.

let the tears stain the paper, a quiet voice inside you will beg like a child
for another chance at this, and you will slam the door;
you've made up your mind.

let the gratitude for your loved ones fill your heart,
and feel the warmth of the love you rejected.
you don't think beautiful things like that could be given to people like you.
they must want something in return because you are undeserving.
notice how some stayed. you take it as they must dislike themselves too,
fall asleep halfway through writing them and watch the sunlight creep
onto your face for the first time in months.

10. wish that it could be enough, and know you could never be.
it was stupid to try.
listen to the tiny urge within you to open the window,
feel the breeze and hear the children laughing.
the world will be the same without you;
see the beauty of it all as you become an observer.
see the light in the children's eyes and recognize the loss of your own.
miss everyone, and wonder where they have gone.
forget that if you reached out, you know you wouldn't be alone.

11. call someone and ask how they're doing.
it's the least you can do, you're leaving now.
open up, talk about it, like a dam breaking down; flood the room,
feel the warmth of their arms around your cold body.
know that it is okay to be okay—you do not have to be sick to be alive.
know that being sick isn't the end, that you are not dead yet,
and you will be okay again.
healing is never linear,
and you are never completely on your own, even in an empty room.
if you feel suffocated, scream, plea to be seen,
take the risk that they might see right through you,
that you might be already too gone to save,
isn't that what you wanted to hear?

12. the world may not change its axis without you,
but someone else's would shatter beyond repair.
if it's all you have then stay for other people, until you can do it for yourself.
do whatever it takes for another day, for one more sunrise and sunset.

you can do it another week, for now.
watch the beauty of the world you live in, for such a short time.
everything will pass.

13. try to observe it as a viewer.
isn't it lovely, how the stars are seen as animals and people
though they're no art we understand?
isn't it beautiful we have art for every human experience nearly,
and for the things we don't have yet, it is being created?

what a gorgeous thing it is to understand, to find something that speaks to
you, without a voice even—a brief conversation with some star-like listener.
you are not alone, and you never have been.
you will stop feeling this way someday,
whether you want it now or not,
the only thing that is forever is death, you are alive.
and as you read this, your heart beats.
your lungs still provide you air, and your hands can still touch things,
and your feet can still carry you.
you might want to leave, but your body will do anything to keep you here;
even if nobody loves you, it still does.
even when you feel like you're alone,
you still can understand yourself.

the week after I killed myself

Monday.
I watched as the time ticked slower and slower.
I could feel my pulse in my hands. I forgot to leave a letter,
and now my parents are left to wonder where they went wrong.

Tuesday.
the news reached my best friend.
I don't know what he does, but I wish I was there to comfort him.
the news comes on, the usual, police chase, the weather,
politics, and the weather, but my parents don't watch.
the tap in the bathroom drips because I forgot to make sure it was fully off,
like I always did.
my mom would tighten the knob for me and
not say a thing until it was the fifth time in a week,
but now she's trying to remember the way I used to wait all year for summer
when we went to the beach, before the move,
before she knew what was happening to me,
back when she thought she could still save me.
the school is notified, my grades don't weigh me down in where I end up,
I don't have to try so hard to matter now.

Wednesday.
the letters in my room are just letters now.
they'll only be read maybe once more, though it'll never be said
how many times they saved a life—I'd hope you knew.
my stuffed animals have not slept in days.
without a cold body to warm what place do they have in this old house?
the neighbors find out, condolences are given,
and not once is my real name mentioned.
my dog wanders through my room
like she did after we got back from a trip with my best friend,
when she sniffed around the entire house looking for him.
the difference is she'll see him once more, and she'll never see me again.
she'll never understand what happened.
she'll never know where I am, or if I'm ever coming back.

leave the light on, when you go

Thursday.
the funeral is arranged for Saturday,
because my mom is always off work then.
I do not know who will come, or what will be said.
I do not know where or how I will be buried.
I was not old enough to pick the arrangements for myself,
knowing my parents I'm probably a diamond or a tree.

the letters have been found. they know.
they know I loved you and you loved me, and I would have joked
about how awkward it'll be when you see my parents again,
but my mom hugs you this time.
she says how she hasn't seen her baby happy like that in years,
and you both forget where you are for a moment.
you dream and hope a little
when you open your eyes it's a different situation.

Friday.
my mom is going through my stuff, my phone first,
she'll find out we were more than friends.
she'll tell my friend that I'm gone, and she won't know if it's a joke,
but when she sees what I've written,
the sinking feeling in her stomach will be all too familiar.
afterwards, my mom will go to the store,
and she'll see the man who always used to ask how I was,
and break down in front of the produce.

Saturday.
the baby's breath is half dead, and the lavender makes the air tense.
there's a mix of regular black clothes and formal wear.
I would've laughed at anyone who bothered to put on a suit
and told you that you look beautiful.
my mom compiled home videos and photos from the last years,
though there are only a few she thinks are really me,
usually, the ones where someone else is with me.
the one with the puppy playing with my hair is one of them.
I didn't have that long hair anymore when I left.
my mother might say the usual: the kind, the smart, the talented,
the too young for this, the brave, her pride or maybe she'd say nothing at all.
maybe she'd ask you if you'd like to say anything,
and I wouldn't be able to hear it.
I always wanted to know what you think of me.

star hands

Sunday.
my room is still like how I left it: coats on the hanger
the boots outside the closet door,
the books dusty and unbookmarked. there'll search for me here,
but none of the words will sound like my voice.
and my mom will keep the video of me as a kid laughing close to her chest.
she wonders where I went when I got older. how was the grave of her baby?
how could I leave her behind after all the things I said without an apology
after all that's been done for me? it was a waste to love me,
I think somebody will think, but I won't be sure.
wherever I am—heaven, hell, nirvana—I won't come back.
I won't be able to run my hands through your hair, and I won't be able to feel
the warmth of another hand to remind me I'm still there.
I won't hear the music, and I won't hear screams or pleas.
I will be at peace, but I'll be nothing more than I am now.

The month after,
my favorite teacher from middle school heard
through an old friend's little sister.
he had gotten me into writing and never saw what it had done for me,
saving me more times than any other person,
giving me a way to explain every feeling I've had since.
my room was cleaned out. my mother took the clothes that fit her
so they wouldn't go to waste, and donated the rest.
she gave my guitars to a friend of mine,
we were planning on starting a band, but the chance is over now.
I can't regret anything, because it will be the same forever.
I'll stay the same age while everyone I love gets older.
I will stay behind in the town we were all running out of,
a memory in a place I never wanted to be.

The year after,
my mom will visit somewhere I wanted to live.
she'll look for me in the little kids passing by
and see nothing except similarities, reminders she is no longer a mother.
sometimes she'll still call out my name looking for me,
or she'll try to text me and see the text turn green.
she will wish I'd just left her on seen like I always did before.
now she can't go into my room without wishing she'd known how to save me,
but there's nothing she could've done; it wasn't her fault,
but she'll spend her life thinking that it is.

leave the light on, when you go

my friends will think a call or a text checking up on me might've saved me,
but probably it would've only postponed it.
but maybe they are right: maybe it would've.
on some warm summer night when I'm convinced I'm alone,
my phone would light up and we'd talk all night.
but that's the thing: this is all in theory.
you didn't believe me then, and you wouldn't until it was already done.

the year after you killed yourself

The year after, I visited somewhere you wanted to live.
I walked along the sidewalks of the houses you swore someday you'd afford.
I look for you in the line of little kids passing by, but I forget
you're no longer as small as them.
I brought you up in conversation, by accident,
and forgot I'm no longer a mother when they asked me how many kids I have,
I said I had just one, and when they asked what your name was,
I said your real one.

sometimes when the day has been busier than my mind can catch
the passage of time, I call out to you to ask what you want for dinner,
but you don't answer so I text you, and instead of leaving me on seen,
the text turns to green.

I can't go into your room now, without wishing I'd just find you crying
instead of an empty bed. I wish you had let me help you,
instead of taking it into your own hands.
you always thought you had to deal with stuff alone,
I wish you weren't so independent now.

there isn't a night I don't spend wishing I had come into your room that night,
I would have rather walked in on you than never see you alive again.

leave the light on, when you go

the week after you killed yourself

Monday. I watch as the hours pass, and I send you a few videos in between
them, but you don't like or respond to any of them.
you don't even leave me on seen.
you haven't opened your phone all day.
I try to reassure myself that maybe you're just out
with your family, or a friend.
but I know you— as forgetful as you are,
you always make time for everyone even on your busiest days,
even when you feel your worst.
you've always hated making others worry.

Tuesday. you still don't answer, and I try to ignore it.
maybe you went through with your plan,
to delete all your socials so you won't be on your phone all the time anymore.
but I can't shake the feeling that something's wrong.
our friends talk shit about some girl we barely know,
and I wish you were here because you're the only one
who will talk about something else or tell them off.
I think of what I'm doing after school.
I think of my new art project, which I haven't told you about yet.
I try to think about anything but you, but it all comes back to you anyway.

you've been absent a lot throughout the year, and when someone asked why,
you laughed and said your mental health got so bad
you couldn't get out of bed.
there have been times when I've looked into your eyes
and I swear I didn't know how you still smiled and laughed.
you looked so tired. at first you were denying it,
saying you were fine when you weren't, but then you stopped,
you admitted it, and nobody knew what to say, so,
our friends changed the subject as you sat there quietly with your head down.
and I sat down next to you and asked you if you walked to walk around,
and we did, that was the first time I ever saw you cry.
you said you didn't think you'd make it to next year, and I said,
"you better at least make it to the day after your birthday, in six months,
I don't want to be older than you."

Wednesday. three days with no response. I haven't seen you at school either.
I asked one of your teachers if you had been there—you used to stay in
classrooms during lunch so, you didn't have to talk to anyone
when things were bad before—but they haven't seen you either.

star hands

they asked me if I knew why you were gone,
and I said that I wish that I knew, but I don't.
there's no message explaining where you've been,
no new poem posted that you forgot to tell me you were working on,
no new news on people you know that I've only met once a few years ago.
I think of texting one of them to ask if they've heard from you,
but I decide to wait until Friday.
I feel weird, unnatural.
maybe it's because I stopped texting you about every little thing.
I think it's anger, but not towards you.

Thursday. I overthink my actions from the week before,
the things you said: *did I upset you, did I make the wrong joke?*
you seemed like yourself the last time I saw you, but you said
when you were going through your worst, nobody suspected a thing.
then, one question comes to mind, it swirls around
outweighing the other possibilities: did you finally go through with it?

Friday. I open my phone at every chime, hoping that I'm wrong.
this time, your name finally appears, but something feels strange.
instead of a text, it's a call. you always called me abruptly,
but I know you wouldn't leave this long without returning
with a paragraph of an apology.

I answer like it's any other time but it's your mom who answers.
she's calling every one of your friends to tell us the news.
I hold on to the chance it's a nightmare I'll wake from,
and I'll see your name pop up, asking myself if I'm still awake
or a reality that feels more like hell because it's one you're not in.

I don't cry, but it feels harder to breathe now.
I blame myself for your death, thinking I could have saved you.
I think, maybe if I had stayed up later that night the week before
your mom wouldn't be crying, and the teachers wouldn't be receiving emails
on why you aren't coming back.
I wouldn't have to explain to the teacher you kept in contact with
since middle school why he hasn't been sent any more of your work.

the gap in my heart will never heal. I won't be able to talk to anyone else
who understands like you did what it is like to feel different.
I think over and over, *what I could've done?*
listened more, reached out more often?

but in every message, I reread for signs,
I swear I can hear you say, "It's not your fault, I chose to do this."
"you couldn't have done anything that would've stopped me.
it'd only postpone it and make us both feel more guilty."
but I feel like you're wrong.

I feel like there's something I could have done before it was too late.

Saturday. at your funeral, there was a mix of formal wear
and black casual clothes. I wore a formal dress,
even though I know you would've laughed at me for it.
your parents brought your dog with them,
and she jumped up onto me and your other friends.
your best friend petted her, and she wrapped the leash around his legs.
your mom hugged him.
they didn't talk much, but I could see the tears in his eyes
start to appear before he turned away and took his seat.
the dog looked around the room during the service,
eyes mainly catching on the picture they had of you.
it was a school photo, and you looked like you didn't want to be there.
I saw you after it was taken, and you said there's no point smiling
since nobody was supposed to see the photo.
I talked to some of your friends, and you were right: we do get along great.
maybe on a different occasion, we could've all hung out.
maybe then we wouldn't feel so alone.

Sunday. your mom goes through your phone
and finds the goodbye letters for your friends.
upon reading mine I finally break. I don't usually cry,
because it's a sign of weakness, and I don't want to
because I don't want anyone to worry about me.
you don't believe in any religion, but I do.
so, if you're there watching me, I'm sorry for the meltdown.

The month after, I explained to your old English teacher that you passed.
he didn't let anyone in his class for a couple of days after that.
someday the thought crosses my mind of how you wanted to be an English
teacher, too, and the students you could have saved if you stuck around.
maybe you could've even saved yourself.
I wonder if you regretted it in your last moments.
did you wish for a minute more? what did you feel?
was it the peace you felt you could never find here?

star hands

you said as soon as you graduated, you'd move across the country.
you hated living in this state
even though it was the only one you had ever known.
I'll think of you every time I come home for Christmas and summer,
and wish I'd pass you in a grocery store, like all our other friends.
at some point, I eventually do go to the thrift store
we talked about checking out, and I saw your stuffed animals there.
I used some of my money to buy two of them.
the lady at the register doesn't know the names you gave them.
they sleep with me in my bed every night.

The year after, I think that a call, a text,
checking up on you might've saved you.
but I can't go back, and I can't wish on anything for a summer night I could,
just one where we'd call and stay up all night.
you'd find a reason to keep you here long enough
you had more to stay than to leave,
or maybe just enough hope for a better tomorrow.
you'd live to watch the sunrise, and see what you made other people feel.
but it's already done, and I can't convince you you're making a mistake.
I only hope that you're happy now,
and I hope that you know someday, I'll be with you.
when I see you again, I'll tell you of the things that have happened
that you would have never believed.

Two years later, I've spent more of my life without you than with you.
I'm older than you now, and I've graduated.
my family's moving cities, not leaving the state, but might as well be.
in the back of my mind any time I read a poem.
I find myself wishing that it was yours, or that I could send it to you;
you were the only one I knew then who liked stuff like that.
sometimes I wonder if we'd still speak all the time if you were still here,
and what my life would be like
if my daydreams weren't the only thing left of you.
would we go to college and live together like we talked about?

leave the light on, when you go

stay another night

eat breakfast. *you can kill yourself tomorrow.*
walk the dog, and read your favorite childhood story. *you can do it next week.*
make plans with a friend, cry tonight like it's the last time you can,
and go to bed.
you can die in the morning.
make brunch. *you can do it at noon.*
pick the flowers and water them, and find a spot you missed on a dish,
and find another on the floor; look at the clock it's three now.
you can do it Sunday.
but your friend invited you for brunch,
and the clouds look like they might rain today.
walk home, and sit in front of the washer until your clothes dry,
stay up until four in the morning, and watch movies
until you forget you were supposed to be dead four weeks ago.
yet you have lived since then—it's a sign
there's still some will in you to go on.
you may not have made it out of the storm completely yet,
but you are still here, and I am sure you will make it to the calm once again.

you have tomorrow to try again

leave the light on, when you go

the day after your partner dies

the morning after your partner dies, you will not wake to the movement of
them in your bed, but the sound of the mourning doves calling.
you will not know for the first few minutes; you'll assume
they're in a different room.

you will faintly feel their hands running through your hair
like they had done the last time you were together.
hear their laughter when you spoke to them sleepily,
just before you both drifted off.
you think of the plans you've made, but the silence will remain,
and you'll remember you're alone.

when you found out, you blamed nobody but yourself.
you know they'd tell you it wasn't your fault, no matter what caused it.
you'd try to be strong, but without them, it's hard to not collapse.
as time passes, your thoughts shift to their family,
the family you were going to be a part of.
but now their hearts have broken apart,
and neither of you can sew the stitches to the wound.

whether you believe in religion or not, you will feel lost,
and you can only hope they aren't anymore.
the hours will feel as if they drag on for days, and the weeks will pass so fast,
that you can't seem to catch up to everyone else.
who had only known them from a few conversations.
you wish you could bring them back, to show them
who they didn't know they were missing.
you're convinced there will always be a part of you missing.

you'll get condolences, but they will never comfort you like they would.
you will hear over and over: *it'll get easier.*
you'll fall in love with someone else.
but you don't think you want to—you don't want to have to lose them twice.
your biggest fear is forgetting them and the love you shared.

you'll see their favorite flowers, movie franchise continue on without them
and a post about the city you had talked about moving together.
you'll see the stars and miss the spark in their eyes you watched drain.
 you'll miss the way they spoke, and you'll replay their voicemails
and videos they sent until you can no longer bear to.
you'll find something they liked at the store and ask if they need more,
but as you press send the text turns to green instead of seen.

six months after your partner dies, you'll go out,
and for the first time, you feel like you can breathe again.
you'll still catch yourself looking for their face in every crowd,
and checking your phone more than you had before you met them,
your heart will sink a little bit each time as you remember
that their name will never come up on the screen again.
people will laugh and smile, kiss and hug.
they'll get married, have children,
and read their wedding vows to each other instead of eulogies.
their family's faces will always be stuck in your mind.
you will keep contact with maybe one of them, probably their mother,
and share the stories they've told of you, and how they felt right this time.
briefly, when you look into their eyes in photos,
you'll still wish to name a kid with their smile
and you're sure they would be just as perfect as them,
but you'll never get to meet them.
you'll think of the pets you wanted to raise together
and sit alone cold in your bed; even with the covers
wrapped around your body, you couldn't feel less lonely.

a couple years after your partner passes,
you will meet another person but won't pursue them.
you will be too afraid to move on
in fear you'll lose what little you have left of them.
you will not have the strength to call them your ex,
so you'll settle for calling them late.
but they were always early to everything,
and now you're living in a world they aren't.
sometimes it still feels like the first week without them.
you will think about them as you knew them a year ago,
and try to imagine the life you would have together if they were still here.
you dreamt you'd grow old together, but someday
you'll have remembered them for longer than you knew them.
you'll get older, but they'll always stay the same age.

you'll miss the little things, the jokes, your show,
the talks and walks; the mornings, nights, and lazy afternoons.
but you also miss all the things you will never have together.
you will never see who they would have grown into,
how their career would turn out, how their self-expression would change.
they will never see who you end up becoming,
how you change, how you stay the same.

you'll blame yourself and think over what you could have said,
or noticed the signs before they made a change you couldn't undo.
the memory has replayed a thousand times in your mind,
but you can find no solution to bring them back.
they're dead, and there's nothing you can do about that.
you feel like it's your fault, it's not.
I can repeat that a thousand times, but only you can accept that for yourself.
it's not your fault, no matter how many nights you lay awake,
trying to convince yourself there is something you could have done.
but it isn't—and wasn't—your fault.

star hands

how to save a life

1. write a poem. be honest, be raw.
you don't have to rhyme—just write what you want.
It doesn't matter if feelings are attached
or if it's just a story that needs to be made.
you don't have to post it anywhere
or write it neatly—you can make a mess and clean it up later.
it doesn't have to be perfect, and no feeling is crystal clear.
it doesn't have to save someone else's life to save one.
you could save future you,
give yourself just another reason to be here another day.
give yourself a release, or a window to a new perspective.
it is worth a try to create art, every time.
if you don't like it, then start over.
if you like it, then don't be afraid to be proud of yourself.
there are no guidelines for art or poetry.

2. check up on your friends. ask them how things are going,
and if they have any plans for the weekend.
or if there is anything they'd like to talk about.
you can't save people, but you can show them you love them,
and that's the closest thing to being a guardian angel, friends can be.

3. pay a compliment to someone—the cashier, the waiter,
your sister, a friend, a stranger, a teacher.
one sentence can stick with someone for a lifetime,
so don't be afraid to be kind.
you can be the change you want to see.
every trend starts with one person, and that person could be you.
be someone you would look up to.
say sorry when you've messed up, say *"thank you, you're welcome,"*
just as one compliment can turn someone's whole day around
so can acknowledgment.

4. pay attention. only drive if you're fully there.
don't check your phone on the road, and don't risk your life and others.
just because you can't wait five minutes to text back,
or at least pull over to the side.
one mistake can and has caused people lifetimes of grief.
pay attention to yourself as well, notice when you start to feel bad,
and reach out for help.

5. ask help when you think you need it,
your problems don't go away no matter how much you ignore them,
no matter how small or how young or old you are,
you deserve care.

6. live your life for yourself, because you're the one
who has to deal with the consequences.
you're the only one who's guaranteed to remember
for the rest of your life what you have done with it.

so make your only chance one you'd wish to live through again.
not to fix mistakes, but because you'd do anything for another day,
and because you made this life something you're afraid to lose.

make your life something that makes death an end.
make your life something that makes you afraid to die,
because if you don't, there won't be any difference between life and death,
except that in death, you'll never get another chance to change things.

star hands

tonight

the floor whispered and held me tighter than any friend I've ever had.
every word I've told you swirled around in my head.
I don't know why I told you to call when I knew even, I wouldn't do it.
all the city lights looked like gifts from angels coming back home;
all the music suddenly was mine in the dark of the night.
I looked at the sky above from my window and I saw the stars
look down at me in disappointment, their constellations dulled,
and I swear I heard the world go silent for a minute.
if I let go now, this could all end, and then what would I be?
another headliner for a week or two if my parents talked enough,
used as an example for a decade on how to look for warning signs.
I thought to myself was this really how it was going to end?
alone on my bedroom floor, with nobody knowing what led to this?
half-assed written letters to my friends that were always there
until I shoved them away?
but there was no amount of reasoning I could give to the voice in my head,
so, I turned out the light, and I hoped tomorrow
wouldn't be the same as tonight.

paris

my friend asked me if I was interested in anyone.
I almost lied to her and told her I thought I was in love
just so she wouldn't have to worry about my mental health anymore,
we talk about suicide as if it's any other topic;
I think we both know we'd never do it,
but we don't look both ways on the street
unless we're holding hands with each other.
she keeps all her locked notes as her birthday in case they find her.
my own letters are handwritten in case they can't figure out my passcode.
we have a playlist we hope they'd play at our respective funerals.
we titled them both Paris: mine for on the way there,
and hers on the way home.

I'll sit in the window seat first and watch the sunrise,
and we'll switch when we leave in the evening
so, she can watch the cities below,
and she'll talk about how someday she'll live there.
and I don't know if we'll ever afford the trip, but we might
if we worked and saved, if we slept through the worst nights,
if we called each other when we ran out of hope in the summer.
maybe if we could save each other enough times, in little ways,
unknowing at the time by just being a friend, we could make it.
and that's enough of a reason for me to stay right now.

star hands

how to fall in love with living again

1. set your clothes out the night before,
and make an outfit you adore, with the bracelets and necklaces,
you didn't have the reason or desire to wear before.
treat yourself like you would a loved one, because you're someone too.
wash your face, brush your teeth, and fix up your hair,
you deserve care just as much as anyone else.

2. when you get up make your bed, tuck in your stuffed animals,
and replace the lightbulb that's almost dead.

3. shower and feel the temperature of the water drip on your skin.
notice the color of the walls and touch your skin:
you are here, and you are safe.

4. make yourself breakfast. it doesn't matter if you're in a rush.
spend a moment completely entranced in it, then get on your way.

5. notice, be present in the moment.
watch the people who you've gone to school with for the last decade
all turn into more than just classmates.
notice who looks down and who has just gotten their laugh back.

6. compliment the people you have always wanted to.
compliment new people on things you've just noticed.
open the door for people, and let someone borrow a pencil,
even if you know you're not going to get it back.
be the change you want to see in the world,
all it takes is one person to change thousands of lives.
small or enormous, everything has a ripple.

7. compliment yourself. notice the beauty in your small actions,
the way you laugh, the way your hair fits your face like a perfect frame.
have empathy for little you—they were doing the best they could.
have empathy for others, for we know so little of other lives.
we only know what other people show us.

8. however, don't let people walk all over you.
you deserve respect as much as they do understanding.
a reason does not equal an excuse, and change is not impossible for anyone.

9. smile at the cashier in the grocery store.
try to go a whole day without saying a mean thing.
hand out a few compliments, and see how you feel by the end of the day.
I guarantee you'll feel better than if you hadn't.
gentleness is infectious, someone just has to be willing to take the risk.

10. if you can go with your friends to a arcade,
give your leftover tickets to a little kid and watch
as their face lights up while they jump around excitedly
because they have enough for that prize they wanted.

11. fall asleep to the idea that any day may be your last.
don't take this as a reason to not do anything at all but rather,
if this was your last day, what's a little embarrassment
as a price to pay to make someone's day?
compliment the intimidating-looking girl,
and say hello to a few more people than you would usually.

12. know that someday you will not wake up, and use that as a reason
to fall in love with your life—you only have so long to know it before it ends.

13. remember that no matter how many people love you,
nobody can make you love yourself but you.
loving others, will not fill what only you can give yourself,
and relationships will not be the cure for what you lack with yourself.
loving someone else can change you for the better,
and it can make loving yourself easier, but you still have to put in the work
to love yourself, even with someone by your side.
it is something only you can do for yourself.

14. you did not come into this world on your own,
nor will you leave it alone, but you are the only one
who will know your life inside and out.
don't be afraid to let yourself trust, love,
and lose—you'll get back up every time.
think of how many things you would have missed out on
if you never had given this life a second chance,
then a third, and then a fourth, and so on.
keep giving yourself these chances, because someday
life won't have any more time for you to try again.

surviving alone is not living, but it is a step in the right direction.
everyone has to start somewhere.

things take time and remember this is only your first time living;
when you were learning to walk you fell countless times.

you're going to make mistakes, but it's not the end of the world.
learn from them, make necessary changes, forgive yourself,
and don't be afraid to apologize.

you still have time to grow; you're still learning until your last breath.

phase

life is just another phase—you're never going to be the same
as you are today.

you'll think about memories that were no more than passing moments.
someday this will just be another one that you think about.
someday, you'll have nobody to keep these stories.
they will all be in the past, without a way to resurrect them.
every moment will be as it was then: happening, happened,
existed, and yet still existing.

the world doesn't know a way without those moments.
no stranger knows what's going on with you.

the stranger you almost complimented
doesn't know anyone else liked their outfit.

assuming everyone else is doing something makes nothing happen.
reaching towards something can change everything,
but staying at the sidelines makes no one aware you're even there.

you can never take back the things you said,
they're on repeat until all the voices stop.

the world will never be the same with you, without you,
you exist, and you have changed the world by being here,
somebody still thinks about you.

indirectly or directly, somebody has seen you, you have seen somebody,
every stranger has parts of the ones they love,
and every stranger has nights they don't want to wake up from.

these phases of life we only see parts of, how they caused this one,
only you will know yourself to completion.

star hands

the day that you finally wake up as yourself

the morning sunlight will spill over you like milk
and wrap you in its warmth like silk.

you'll open your eyes, and the first thing you will notice
will not be the heaviness of your heart.

it will be the morning birds chirping; you could hum along
if you listened for long enough.

the bedsheets will be tangled, and the first thing you think about
when you think of your body will not be your weight or the scars.
you will not wish that you hadn't woken up.

instead, for a brief moment, you will feel some sort of gratitude.
it's faint, but enough to brush a gentle smile across your face.

the day will wash over you like a tide to sand.
you'll wake up and splash some cold water on your face,
and your day will start without a feeling of regret haunting,
you from the night before.

time will seem to pass more smoothly,
someday you'll feel less like a ghost, and your house will feel like a home.
just give yourself the time and try your best when you can.
some days your best will just be your survival and that'll be enough.

leave the light on, when you go

ACKNOWLEDGMENTS

Thank you to my English teachers in the last few years who have changed my life by getting me interested in writing again.

Thank you to my friends and family who always supported my work even as a little kid and every friend I have made in process of creating this book, nothing would be the same without all of you.

Thank you to everyone who has given me platform to show my work.

Thank you, Tara Maggs, for editing this book and sharing your writing excises with me and others, I can't wait to see what you do with your talent.

Made in the USA
Middletown, DE
10 September 2024

60682273R00050